MAK

MAKESHIFT ALTAR

poems

AMY M. ALVAREZ

UNIVERSITY PRESS OF KENTUCKY

A note to the reader: This volume contains references to sensitive topics, including historical and contemporary instances of racial oppression. Discretion is advised.

Published by the University Press of Kentucky,
scholarly publisher for the Commonwealth, serving Bellarmine University, Berea College, Centre College of Kentucky, Eastern Kentucky University, The Filson Historical Society, Georgetown College, Kentucky Historical Society, Kentucky State University, Morehead State University, Murray State University, Northern Kentucky University, Spalding University, Transylvania University, University of Kentucky, University of Louisville, University of Pikeville, and Western Kentucky University. All rights reserved.

Editorial and Sales Offices: The University Press of Kentucky
663 South Limestone Street, Lexington, Kentucky 40508-4008
www.kentuckypress.com

Cataloging-in-Publication data is available from the Library of Congress.

ISBN 978-0-8131-9902-3 (hardcover : alk. paper)
ISBN 978-0-8131-9903-0 (paperback : alk. paper)
ISBN 978-0-8131-9904-7 (epub)
ISBN 978-0-8131-9905-4 (pdf)

This book is printed on acid-free paper meeting
the requirements of the American National Standard
for Permanence in Paper for Printed Library Materials.

Manufactured in the United States of America.

Member of the Association
of University Presses

For my family:
those who left, those who stayed, those who are yet to come.

For myself at five, at seven, at fifteen, at nineteen.
Here we are. Here you go.

Home is neither here nor there. Home is within you, or home is nowhere at all.

—HERMAN HESSE

Contents

III

Skin

I try to resemble my family:
each a shade of Jupiter's swirl,
one of us always the storm.

Born with obeah on our backs;
orisha traverse our dreams.

Pantheons bud from our brows—
trinities to dozens-playing demi-deities.

Let survivors' bones grow fat with sweet.
Let me honey up the fire lilies.

We are fragmented here; colonization
dicing some more finely than others.

Come, holy skin, bring your voices
to this new land: virus-quiet, heart-valve loud.

Forced to dance in scarcity, I eat what
you eat: stringy mango of absence.

Sirius came to the Egyptians before flood.
Survival: blossoms buried in mud.

I

Appalachia → LGA

Through double plexiglass panes, I trace
   swollen river inlets & muddy deltas.

White smoke flowers from the mouths
   of bottom-heavy smokestacks. In West Virginia,

by god, I feel the boundary of dense green
   woodland, willowy fingers on my gasping throat.

But I am not of these mountains. I am Queens
   concrete, endless signs in every alphabet, from

subway cars and women therein who weep,
   who hold on to yellow grocery bags while the 7

screeches along track's edge. I map a path
   back to my mother & her mother: one purging

her life of detritus—old LPs, books she will
   not read, husbands—& the other's urge to hang

on to it all—her horde of VHS tapes, featuring
   nations she will never see, for fear of flying, form

a wild topography in her hallway. I follow the line
   back from Flushing & Laurelton out to that first

Jamaica, sunken Redbirds snaking an undersea
    railway stretching from Queens to plantation heat

in Kingston, in St. Ann's Parish, out to an avenue
    named for my French Catholic forefather who crossed

himself after coming in my Yoruba foremother.
    I dare myself to return, to want this return, cloud
    quiver above ocean reef, skirting the continent of what is.

Morgantown

The list of Wi-Fi networks in our neighborhood runs from FuckPad
to Xfinity. Across the street, a chained dog won't stop barking.

It's cold, and he whimpers like a child. Maybe it's the train's whistle
that upsets him. We're far from needing the warning in this bed,

smelling of fabric softener and the soft pepper of cats. Trains
carry the coal that brings back the money that state politicians use

to gussy up the now-flooded golf course they frequent, hire
some university professor with dusty books she can't part with.

Little is spent on miners' black lung, on their shattered
children, tracks on their arms forming maps of constellations
they'd like to become someday.

Dominant/recessive

i.

Spit in a tube. Wait. Wait for a list of diseases you might pass
on to future generations, for a chart focused on forty-six slivers
of fragmented past.

ii.

Four hundred and sixty generations ago, my mitochondrial
mother strode Central African plains. She stroked stars with
Bantu songs.

iii.

Cristóbal Colón—devil in explorer's pantaloons—called Taínos
"shapely of body . . . handsome of face." He hacked off their hands
before the Spanish named Borinquen Puerto Rico, before Xaymaca
became Jamaica. Gilt veins of their survival thread through my own,
shards of their language still strewn across our tongues—canoa,
barbakoa, Juracán.

iv.

Casta paintings showed Spanish monarchs what happened
when their sailors mated with Indians and, later, with Africans.
Paintings featured mixed families: man, woman, child.
They suspected European blood would scrub color clear after
a few generations. When African blood did not disappear,
they named the children mulatto, lobo, cochino, albarazado.

They named them no te entiendo, tente en el aire, worthless.
Then they stopped painting.

v.
Somehow, we have survived: a line of un-toca-bles. Double helix
of stardust fallen over whatever land we found after sea.

vi.
Scattered ancestry paints a colorful quilt of chromosome across
my computer screen. A heterozygous history, one of many possible
outcomes.

vii.
I tire of trying to decipher the patterns of history.
I stand outside, study her same stars, and sing.

Eleggua

Last night, I dreamed Eleggua
dancing by the sea. He dressed in white,
wore a straw hat. He reflected sun

back to itself. Momentarily mortal—
a lump of clay like the rest of us—
he picked up cowrie shells by night,

fished by day, singing *ago ile*,
ago, dancing—always listening
for the hum of Yemayá in the tide.

He danced equivocating drums,
reminder that we are all the sainted
sinner, the lost found.

———*///*———

My great-grandmother hid her orisha
behind lapis-robed saints.
Her husband smashed her altars,

but she still performed ceremonies
in the womb of night—a chicken
offered as sacrifice to protect a sick

child, a song to ask Eleggua to make
a way where there was none.

Little Church

the bass is deep

      & occasional

            like the voice of god

in the midst of electricity
              a whistle

                          sound of wet human lips
              beckons us

                        out of the dark

duality of puckered mouth

          & miles davis' high-voltage horn

                          fill the empty space

as the organ bubbles up underneath

            lush as the spirit in us

                      on the day we were born

on the day we'll up and leave

Cebu City

The monsoon sun rises at four. Long-legged
roosters strut and bellow on sight. I suppose
I am glad to see its light reflected in the bucket
of cold water I use to wash. My own heat steams
the small, cracked bathroom window. The view:
a concrete wall with shimmering shards of broken
glass embedded at the top—a problematic prism.
I go to the market in a purple jeepney named
Martinez. Eight centavos to ride inside where
a placard reminds: *Show your love to JESUS—*
NO SMOKING. We bounce past motorcycles.
A baby vomits on his mother's legs. The jeepney
passes the statue of some Spaniard killed in beds
of coral that surround this island—a burning necklace.

Queensborough

Any version of home I might own
begins not in a room but the backyard
where I first learned the names of flowers:
iris, forsythia, lily.

The house was white with a clay tile roof.
I earned my scars falling out of its crabapple
tree, driveway tumbles on roller skates.

My grandmother wasn't allowed in our house
because of the pain she'd inflicted on her daughters,
but I remember watching her walk up and down
the sidewalk on an August day, full of her own
madwoman power.

I'd go outside to talk to her. She'd give me a stick
of mint gum, her makeup melted in the heat.

She was wearing a purple dress, maybe the same
one my mother said she wore to my parents'
marriage. *I mourn your terrible mistake,* she told
my mother on her wedding day as my father's
Boricua family celebrated. *I mourn your terrible mistake.*

Any version of home must begin
from the outside in, from the Caribbean
to New York, from the melanin in my skin
to my heart muscle pumping in Patois, Spanglish,
in all the Englishes I have inherited, my colonized
tongue perched in the eaves of my mouth.

Hood Aesthetic

Naturally, broken glass, throbbing bass, a roll of bills and a paper bag passed between the hands of hustlers. Just as true: the rows of corn planted by the family at the end of the street. Even in this leaded soil, stalks grow fat cobs. The squeal and clatter of barefoot children chasing each other on asphalt, tight braids flying, shoes abandoned at the back door, rounds of *happy birthday to ya!* from an open apartment window, the shuffle of sneaker and swish of net from the basketball players beneath. In the morning, I step outside to starlings, wings like oil slicks, construction and the smell of hot tar releasing a wavering haze of heat. I wave to a neighbor sitting on the stoop, shirtless, smiling. What neither of us knows is that he will be dead a year from now. His body will lie at the front steps of our building. His dreadlocks will splay across concrete. Another makeshift altar erected at the lamppost on the corner: candles, silk flowers, laminated pictures, empty liquor bottles. But for today, Al Green's falsetto wafts across the street as the blue faces of cornflowers overwhelm the empty lot where a building once burned, as August clutches us to her chest, leaving us slick with possibility.

Easter, 1986

I was boredom bound in lace. My mother tried to save
our souls: mass, half Latin, a white priest in gold
vestments Sunday after Sunday:

                  peace be with you   *and also*

that day was no different. Jesus hung bloody behind
the priest. Reason we came here: his hangdog face,
bloody even on Resurrection Sunday,
still dying, despite the   *aaalleluia*

Make a ham, my grandmother commanded, but I'd never liked
eating pigs, and my mother never liked to cook, so it was bun
and cheese from Mrs. Lee's Jamaican bakery, beef patties
with coco bread, cold Ting and Kola Champagne.

Our mouths stung from scotch bonnet pepper, our souls wiped
clean with holy, my mom, laughing for once, cold monkey bars
behind my knees, hanging upside down, a sky of tree roots and
parked cars, a ground of gray cloud to fall into.

149th Street

The psychic on the corner totes grocery bags past neon
signs in her windows, run in her stocking inching up shin.

I scooped garter snakes from sidewalk cracks. My cats
captured cicadas—fluttering green jewels in their pink mouths.

That corner always needed a streetlight:
boy's blood on asphalt given as testimony.

It isn't lost on me that our expressway was named Utopia.
There never was any question, was there?

I can still see sunset behind the church steeple.
Above juniper's canopy: magenta sky and crows, crows, crows.

Blessed Are the Merciful

Sunday morning, her arms wave high
like she's at church, only she's on the stoop
across from your building, and it's Marvin Gaye
she's swaying to. You don't know her name.

The man who owns the stereo blaring
"Mercy, Mercy Me," shouts from inside
for her to get off his steps. *Now, woman!*
Woman. You have heard her called *crack lady*,
crazy bitch, and *in need of salvation*.

Last night, she slept slumped over
the chain-link fence next door, as our teen
neighbors drank Hennessy and Heineken
their mom bought them, laughed, took pictures.
Her haphazard worship is a marked improvement.

As you walk past her, toward your green Cavalier,
you jingle through your five keys, but she sees you,
and you hear her flip-flopped shuffle. She closes
in—*Hi!*—and there's a hand on your arm, polish
peeling, she smiles, and you see a missing tooth,
her braids half undone, her dirty green T-shirt.
I need to get to the train and these buses too damn slow,
you know?

And you do. It's why you learned to drive
at the laughable age of twenty-six. *Can you
gimme a ride?* You see her jaundiced eyes,
the fresh scab above her left brow.

You were on your way to the grocery store,
pharmacy, a quick trip to get those shoes—
half off today only. You feel the leaden weight
of keys. You wonder what you are waiting for.

The Other Mothers

after Angela O'Donnell

The other mothers were dignified, proper.
Stockings without polish-patched runs, crisp suits.

My mother was a little late, in fuchsia sweatpants,
my forgotten lunch / band uniform / essay in hand.

The other mothers were stay-at-home, never learned
to drive, brought covered dishes to the potlucks.

My mother was revved engine and *shithouse!*
after being cut off. She was twelve-hour hospital shifts,
scalded pot, rock-hard falafel, Chinese food, cold pizza.

The other mothers could crochet and knit, ironed
the sheets, hummed as they vacuumed.

My mother held nails in her mouth, smelled of varnish.
She hissed at the piles of *bombaclaat* laundry that she
worked like *a god-damned dog.* Her worksong: smack
of hampertop, stomp of stair, whir of washer.

Other mothers rushed their children to the ER
after a fall, turned their plump
faces away from the bleeding.

My mother was the savior of trapped baby squirrels,
hacker of lizard tails, splint-maker, *better by tomorrow*
soother, she sucked her teeth at foolishness, looked
at everyone and saw a story.

Rolling

It started early. In my childhood dreams,
I would be alone in my mother's car
and it would roll, backward, downhill. My screams
were soundless. I hit the horn, but fast, far
the white Subaru slid, and would not stop.
I clawed at the upholstery, but the door,
jammed on rusted hinges, would not unlock.
I jolted awake, utterly unmoored.
Even now, stopped at the crest of a hill,
waiting for the light to change, I can feel
my car give, roll gently backward, until
I hit the gas and beg the wound to heal.
I move forward, shift past the purple beech,
forgive myself, shake off dreams, and go teach.

Mont Lawn Camp

The cabin was filled with screaming brown girls
from the Bronx. The bat flapped membranous
wings, collided with campers, wood-paneled walls,
and fluorescent bulbs, refused to be flushed out
of the open window with clipboard or broom.

How could I explain to frantic nine-year-old
campers that the bat would not suck blood
from their bodies or that the long-legged
thing clattering down rocks in the woods
as we marched back from the mess hall
that night was not a wolf but a deer—*see
the velvety antlers?*

How could I help them not fear the sound
a raccoon's slow waddle makes in the dark?
How could I, when back at home the turning
of a handle or a shadow in the window is worth
an electric shriek?

I collected the girls in the living room to wait
for maintenance and asked them to watch it—
the bat's manic attempts at escape, the beauty
of erratic flight. *You're brave*, I said to the girls.
You'll live, I said.

II

In Virginia,

in late autumn before
the ice dazzles, while
the world is still
quiet of color, you
may see the ghost
of a brown woman,
her breath ragged,
cross bare fields. You
may see her race
river, double back, and
climb into tulip poplar's
embrace. She might pound
acorns into a semi-edible
paste. Under pine needles'
gossip, you may hear
her sing starlight, you
may hear a dog
howl, you may watch
your own hands wane
transparent.

Spring Semester

The lanky brown boy who walks ahead of me
wears a red leather jacket so new I can hear it creaking.
Hip Hop rasps tinny through his oversized headphones.

His head bobs as the music comes to the place
where he thinks he knows the words and lets spill:
Shots fall, man down—it's a homicide. He mumbles
as these lyrics fade, a brutal half-haiku.

These are the last words he will utter
before he slips through the blue doors
ahead, begins another day of high school.

Red buds push from maple branches. We
tread over ice and salt. Our path
is narrow—slick and steep.

Search: American Education

paper-filled desk, now a quadrangle of light, now void.
book beats glock outside of crossfire. within it, only speed.

america was patterned on the english system, a two-track
model—one running the inside track, the other shoeless,
rounding the corner.

did you mean *american education broken?*

children went to school under guard; children dodged rotten
fruit, children dodge bullets. shifting sands of time bring

an ancient practice a new name, but funds
are only spent on too-concise history books.

a rumble that grows into a roar:
this is how it begins.

Monongahela Means Falling

In memory of Arthur Bagenda

On the long bridge across river   I pause at lilac

sniffing a story   about a Black boy who

may have fallen   may have been flung

from this height   here: the crowning jewel

of the coal state   college town priding

itself on peace   occasional quiet I find

myself quaking   with grief for his family

for all of us   who share his skin

here: confederate   bumper stickers are equal

to those that remind us   to #Resist

I meditate on a peace   that wears a Black beret

will kneel for an anthem   that rhymes *slave*

with *grave*   at river bottom

crows and hawks   dive bomb the water

for prey arcing a long line   of misery

that mutters   the name of a boy

named for a hero king   I toss a bundle

of lilacs down   say his name

Lighting candles on my stoop / watching the wind snuff them out

I keep thinking about Breonna / asleep between fresh sheets / I keep thinking about her skin cooling after a shower / hair wrapped in a satin bonnet / I wonder what she dreamed that night / I wonder about her bedroom / whether she had painted it recently / argued with her partner about undertones in the paint / this one a little more blue/ this one more pink / I wonder whether she may have felt more at home now that she had chosen the color on her walls / I keep thinking about how she could use her hands to keep blood moving through a human heart / how her hands could stanch the flow of blood until platelets arrived / I wonder how many times she heard / *thank you for saving* / *please save* / *save me* / I wonder how many nights she could / I keep thinking about her when I lie in bed / when I wake up and look in the mirror / when I walk to my front door / I wonder about the life she wanted to build / whether she had her eye on a ring and was dropping hints to the man who chose to protect her / whether it was already in his sock drawer as he waited for the right time / I keep wondering why a black woman's death alone can't begin the revolution / whether the smoke rising to the heavens across this nation is offering enough

Eight Minutes, Forty-six Seconds

have you knelt on hot
asphalt in summer ever
your knees indented
by gravel or another's
flesh & did your hips /
knees / ankles / calves
ever indicate it was time
to shift change position

or get the hell up?

to kneel for nearly nine
minutes is a feat of wrath
& discipline—how much
must you hate your own body

or the neck cradling your patella
to stay there as every tendon
& sinew in your body says
as the being beneath you says
they cannot breathe?

CPR

after Julia Kasdorf

I learned from my mama the best way
to help the dying was to keep courage
close in case someone needed CPR
a crowd gathering
fearful tears gathering

I learned to compress chests with
hands small enough to reach between
wall and dresser for a missing bobby pin
I learned to breathe lifesaving breaths
to wipe saliva flecks with a fingertip

I learned to push through chaos
to occupy the worried hands
of the bystander
to ask for them to call for help
I gathered that whatever I did could fail
that what others might realize is I tried

I fought to think I had the ability to heal
bloody wounds like some saint
some bruja

I learned to make from another's pain
my own valor and once I could do this

to press onward

              and so to every terror

I offer my hands
a scarf as tourniquet
a shout to clear the area
my life's breath

I Am Whatever You Think

I am whatever you
think American is.

That is: monolingual chaos.
That is: eagle-hummingbird falling
from sandstone, rising from ground-
water.

I am whatever you think.
I am whatever.
I am: you think?

I am American
as whatever, as if.

I am exactly what you think I am:
spike to the head of hegemony,
a hurricane on your coastline,
the dust storm willing the ground
to shift under your feet.

Polaris

maybe in the moments before police yelled
gun gun gun maybe before the lead flew into
the soft of his body   Stephon Clark heard
cricket song
maybe he heard his own heartbeat   maybe
he gazed into the dark and found it   lovely
maybe he searched for the Big Dipper and
found the North Star spilling from its brim

An Old White Woman Touched My Hair at Rising Creek Bakery

She asked if it was real and then her hand,
already on its way, brushed my left
shoulder.

The woman was Wearing-a-Sweater-and-
Long-Pants-on-a-Ninety-Degree-Day years
old. This does not excuse her.

This does not excuse me for saying nothing,
for my forced smile and flight. The only
other black woman in the bakery had her
hair under a scarf (all the ways we protect
ourselves).

The old woman's hair was spiked, sparse,
silvery. Should I have touched her strands
as she reached for mine? We could have
stood there, fondling each other's hair
until my spouse, finished with the restroom,
until her grandson, finished with his order,
came to untangle us.

Predatory Rites

in this poem the speaker
captures a silver piranha
on a bamboo fishing pole
using raw meat as bait.

in this poem, the fish is a metaphor
for the poet's mother, for the poet
herself. the fish is Elizabeth Bishop.

the bait is a metaphor for capitalism.
you are a metaphor for capitalism.

the fish bleeds as it emerges
from the river. it is the first time
the speaker has caught a fish.
she wonders who will taste whom.

poet's teeth and piranha's teeth:
metaphors for salt in a pre-
existing wound.

the speaker watches the river
guide pull up a water hyacinth
stem, thick and fleshy as a thumb,
wiggle it between the dying
fish's needle teeth:

in this poem, you are fish and
water hyacinth. in this poem, you
are hinge, piranha's jaw,

you bite clean through.

Boondocks:

─────────────╫─────────────

from the Tagalog *bundók* & Cebuano *bukid*:
each meaning mountain, rurality, folded-up
land far from ocean, from Proto-Austronesian
bunduk: higher ground. When American

soldiers menaced the Philippines after
the nation declared independence from Spain,
Filipinos used bundók as cover, descending
on an army used to prairies, to brown faces

protecting sacred ground raging across
open field instead of behind trees raining
fire down the bundóks. These soldiers
birthed the bastard word *boondocks*

in these mountains, migrating meaning
toward remote country, hinterlands
where the people, in their estimation
(and what is the estimation of a nineteen-

year-old American worth?), were less
civilized or civil. I imagined a boondock
being watery wasteland and didn't expect
it to mean *mountain* in my stepfather's

first tongue or in Cebuano, Cebu being part
of the archipelago I know well from my time
with church folk who proselytized to the choir,
molding Protestants of Catholics, but also

running clinics, providing materials to teachers,
inviting young trans women to hang out, delight
in sisterly love. I met my first out trans friend
in Cebu at fifteen;

she taught me the Cebuano word
for cockroach as a gag: *uk-ok*. *Bakla*
is Cebuano for gay man and transwoman.
bakla   bukid   beauty   bundók

Jennifer Laude was a bakla, Filipina beauty
murdered by American marine in a bathroom
stall because his own desire was distasteful
to him. He could not understand the forests

of her bundóks. The murderer was released
after five years of a ten-year sentence. He—
and I don't bother naming the man from
the boondocks because names are themselves

honorifics—had AC in his cell, was paid a quarter
of a million dollars while he twiddled the thumbs
that held Jennifer's head in a toilet. The US military
remained in the Philippines in exchange for vaccines.

————————///————————

Babaylan: from the Austronesian *balian*—
a word for shaman from the precolonial

Philippines. A babaylan was almost always
a woman like Jennifer: shamans by nature,

guided by spirits of ancestors who brought
them back to their bodies after traveling
to astral boondocks until colonizers drove
them into the mountains. I wish a medium

beyond words to guide Jennifer back to her
body. I wish an army of bakla babaylan:
beautiful, fearless, thundering down
the bundóks, fire streaming from their painted lips.

On Flying over the Border Wall

This morning, a girl dies of dehydration
as she tries to cross the border I fly over.

I gaze at Orion through pergola slats. I grip
guilt tight as the plastic water bottle in my hand.

On our way to Mayan pyramids, a highway
island's stone snake rears its head, its body

entwined in bougainvillea. Obsidian, the shaman
says, is the frozen blood of the planet.

Inheritance

A room with deep blue carpet, mostly
empty. We are moving, leaving this house
for another. I play with a red balloon
and hear my parents shouting downstairs.
I know this shouting is and is not about me.

When I appear at the top of the stairs,
I am told to go back to the empty room.
Instead, I sit with my back pressed
to the wall, neck owl-swiveled
at the banister, to watch and listen.

My father wants me to stay overnight
with him and his new girlfriend, her
two kids close to my age. I like the older
girl especially—she is tall, cool, and can
color inside the lines.

My mother is afraid I will not return.
My father wants more than an eight-
hour visit. I am their only child.

They fight by the front door. Bright
light frames their faces—my mother's
weeping face, my father's face shadowed
by his wildly gesticulating hands, and in

this light, in this quarrel over my body.
I peer from the top of the staircase,
unraveling the shouts that might mean
they love me.

Soil

one letter away from *soul*
and last night i dreamed
you and i moved again,
bringing all our plants
with us. soil from Boston,
Morgantown, soil in pots
our mothers gave us: mint
from New York, lilies from
Virginia. we brought our souls
to this new place and made
it our own: digging down
to mycelium, remixing
notions of home.

On the Futility of Pouring Water on a Dying Dolphin

It is water's nature to take on the shape of its vessel,
to become the orange metal pail, the blue plastic
bucket with turrets for a castle.

I saw the gray back and arc of fin break the waves,
watched the body tilt, rocking side to side. It washed
ashore, blowhole open then shut, then foam, then
nothing. Its tail was frayed along the edges, bleeding.

We poured sea on the back of this dolphin.
The police showed up and instructed us to keep
the dolphin moving so it can breathe. *You keep
a shark moving, not a dolphin*, I told him. *Whichever.*

Flags move like water—now wrinkled, now
smooth, now violent in the wind. Water fills
and takes, is monstrous. Like the shark we
watched attack the dolphin before it washed
ashore. Like us, worrying the shoreline here,
like us, born of water, but not of it any longer.

III

Jíbara Negra

This is how it begins:
with my mother born
in Spanish Town, with
my father born in
Ponce. I was born
on the island of
Manhattan, my
umbilical cord
buried in a midtown
dumpster. We are
all island people,
even if I sound like
a gringa, sound like
I am from farin.

I'm a city girl, but
my parents taught
me to be a jíbara—
at home on horses,
in tents, en el campo,
with dirt under my
nails from the garden,
with my hands curled
around a lizard's tail.

Daughter

For you, the divorce
is a shifting between
suburb and housing
project, burnt lunch
and cannabis smoke,
Sunday morning sermon
and Saturday evening
double Dutch.

You drift in and
out of the arguments
your parents, step-parents,
half- and step-siblings
have in Spanish, Tagalog,
Jamaican patois, the cool
shit talk you don't
hear at private school.

You try to decipher
the sound that love
makes, immigrant
lullabies beating time
on your eardrums.

Shaped into a Kind of Life

A Golden Shovel after Lucille Clifton

After a beating, chest heave, and an *I won't*
do it again sung through gritted teeth spelling *I hate you.*
After, I could count the welts and celebrate—

I still had breath to sob, didn't I? With
my mother/aunt/uncle's mantra *this hurts me*
more than it hurts you dripping from what-

ever belt, brush, shoe, spatula, I
had put into their hands to have
them imprint object on my me. I, shaped

by hands that could bake or bruise, shaped into
compliant child, seen and not heard, a
bud of rage began to blossom. A kind

of blaze, of scissored heat beneath scalp, of
jaw clenched, breeched nuclear core of a life.
I caught the memo: anything weak was target. I

remember grabbing the little girl's wrist, I had
no gentle in my glare. I quaked with the fear in her. No
longer object, but an actor—I could give pain. Model-

ing myself momentarily after de Sade, cruelty born
of soulless ribcage, heavy stomach, broccoli in
her teeth still, eyes brimming. I brought her to my Babylon.

Fly

The summer I turned thirteen,
my Jamaican grandmother
came up from Florida, ushering
in a blight of flies. They roamed
the house in ever-shifting clusters,
outwitting swatter and fist. I felt
guilty killing one with my math
textbook—her ochre insides
smeared on the bedroom window.

My grandmother hauled five suitcases
full of new clothes she bought for us
that she thought were fly, then asked
my mother to pay her bills.

She nagged me about biting my nails,
about dressing *like a man, a hoodlum.*
She insisted my stepfather was a child molester,
was sure my baby sister would die of thirst.

That summer, my Jamaican grandmother
flew straight for me: *I see you into all this
rap nonsense. Just make sure whoeva you
bring home, that there's some cream in
his coffee. You hear? Or just drink milk!*
She laughed too loud, too long.

With straight hair and your features,
you look Indian, pure Indian, she said,
swatting a fly.

All summer, my grandmother slept
in my bedroom. She muttered every
night about the Michael Jordan poster
over my bed: *I don' like that black man*
watching me undress. Chuh. Why you
got to have him up on de wall?

There was no explaining how fly
Jordan was or how wack it all was:
flies circling my head in the heat,
the scent of mothballs in my room,
my grandmother's skin-whitening
cream on the bedside table.

Chiba

My father called me chiba, mi primer hijo—
tomboy, my first son—knuckling the crown
of my head, he said I sat too mannish—

my knees splayed, forearms on thighs,
watching the Knicks on the couch
in his apartment. When I began my model-

plane phase, he came to my mother's house
to help me build an A-10 bomber—each piece
primordial green. We labored over landing gear,
inhaling foul rubber cement.

He mentioned boyhood dreams of building planes,
watching the work of his hands soar instead of clunking
to life like the radiators and refrigerators he worked on.

I told him I was proud of how he fixed what was broken.
My father half-smiled before burying himself in silence
and instructions. We added decals, painted a shark-
toothed mouth on the plane's snubbed nose.

Photo of My Brother in Djibouti

He sits in a foxhole—a shell-shaped depression
in sand with rocks piled on the rim. An automatic
rifle with an enormous scope is held up to his boy
face. The light tells me it is sunrise. His uniform
covered in sand, smile in his eyes, his mouth void.

According to the blurb, he is *manning a defensive
fighting position in East Africa during a strong point
defense training exercise.* This is the first time I
have seen my brother holding a gun. Our mother
never allowed toy weapons (*too violent*, she would
say), so he made them from sticks, Legos, clay,
from cardboard tubes and electrical tape.

Online, the comments section below the image
is filled with platitudes from strangers, thanking
my brother for his sacrifice and service. There
is advice, *use sandbags instead of rocks*, and criticism,
doesn't look like much of a fighting position to me.
His civilian friends tease *did you Photoshop this?*
His army friends say he's *Badass! #SAVAGE.*

In his bedroom at home, dusty taekwondo
trophies, a Bible, Sun Tzu's *Art of War*
and piano sheet music litter the top of his
dresser. Last year at Christmas, he taught

himself "Maple Leaf Rag" and "Silent
Night." He played both songs, loudly,
for whoever would listen.

Before he left, he found the flag that covered
our grandfather's casket, unfurled it from its fifty-
year triangle, hung it on the only wall in his room
without windows. In the back of his open closet lie
the remains of his childhood arsenal—tape peeling
off, the wood splintered—but still, somewhat, intact.

Old Gods

My mother left the Catholics. Kneeling
lost to the ecstasy of tongues. Born-again,
she discarded all she had from her old life.

First came the albums—conglomerate
of her American teendom—The Doors,
Joan Baez, Dylan, The Beatles—all

left out on the wet curb alongside malas
from the time she almost became a Hare
Krishna. She emptied a crate of objects

I'd never seen before: icons in yellow,
green, and brown tossed out in a box
next to the records. From her grandmother's

altars, *for her witchcraft* she said. I asked if
I could take just one record—I'd liked
the cover of *Sgt. Pepper*—just one statue—

the one with glittering eyes. She sighed.
It was all unclean. Through the window,
I watched as cardboard boxes drank rain.

Gloria, In Excelsis

The last time I saw my grandmother, Gloria, her ghosts brought her
to a New York night club. It was 3:35 p.m. on a twenty-first-century
Tuesday, but for her it was 1945 and midnight. She was in a hospital
bed in her living room, a wheelchair beside her. She asked me if I
knew any torch songs. *That's what they come to hear! If you really want
to be a singer, get gigs, you have to learn the songs the people want to hear,
man.* She'd forgotten again that my sister was the singer, that I was
the poet, the failed musician. My husband brought an alto sax to
her house. He knows all the torch songs. He played her out-of-tune
piano until its clang bothered her, and she told him to drag out an
electric keyboard. As she remembered song lyrics, she asked for a
pen and paper to write them down. She beat time on the hospital
bed railing.

I remember you
dyed hair under silk scarf, mint
bulging from garden.

When I was thirteen, my grandmother gave me a copy of Flaubert's
Madame Bovary. I found it dull and gave up. When I had to read it
in college years later, I understood the gift of the book, understood
the gifts that allowed her to navigate a text I struggled with despite
her sixth-grade education. I still wonder why she gave me so many
things in blue when I was a child. It's never been my color—but
every robe, pajama set, blouse, church dress was blue. Flaubert's
lady in blue died. Perhaps she wanted me to know that.

Under mango trees,
you saw your sister's soul in
yellow butterfly.

My grandmother ascribed the old meaning to colors: purple was death. This is why she wore a purple dress to my mother's first wedding, told her she was in mourning before the cake was cut. Green, my favorite color, symbolized envy and greed to her, not chlorophyll and life as it does to me. It was not a color to be worn at all. Black was death. This is why she painted all of the mahogany furniture in her house white and pastel peach and purple when her sisters began dying. She would not live in a house of mourning. She is a Leo, and gold is her favorite color. She would spray paint old mirrors and picture frames with gold. She wore gold kitten heels as house shoes in her eighties. There was nothing wrong with gold—it was wealth, success, power without the greed of green. She never wore blue.

There's a ghost's chance you
might come back as thrush or dove—
something that sings *home*.

Aerodynamics

When I say, *my parents*
 met on a plane, what I
  mean is my existence
  is airborne, what I
   mean is I am not *from*
   from here, that my parents,
   my family, still hover
   above an Americanness
   none of us can fully know,
    that we have been, are right
    now being, reborn as American,
    as Caribbean, as the tear shape
    of a plane's wing, as propeller,
    as immigrant, as dreamer,
   as blue, as black, as brown,
   as success, as failure—
   as if
   this country's constitution,
  its manic manifesto, was folded
  into a paper plane that landed
  right on Sally Hemings's lap
 and she tossed it to Louverture,
to Sharpe, to Albizu Campos,
as if we belonged here, as if we
were meant to survive, as if,
as if.

IV

How to Date a White Boy

1.

Do not be his melanated test drive.
You are no one's enigma
or experiment. Find evidence: an old
photo online or in a dusty shoebox
under his bed. Do not feel flattered.

2.

If you meet his parents, prepare
for disappointment. You will want
them to be pleased with your philosophy
thesis / your grandma's pearls. You will
hope they are immediately rude so you
don't waste another fertile year on their son.
They will invite you to a cookout (they will
call it a barbecue, but it will be a cookout).
Don't get upset when you overhear
the grandmother say you are darker / smarter /
prettier / more or less articulate than expected.
She will be dead before the wedding.

3.

So, you've fallen in love. Remind him
before you create a joint Instagram,
before you adopt a shelter dog,
that you wear the same MAC foundation

number as Sandra Bland, that your brother
looked like Tamir when he was little.
Before you argue names for imagined children,
remind him what could happen to a boy
with your face.

4.
So, your white boy thinks you should move
in together. Take him to ungentrified Bronx
neighborhoods where old men play dominoes
on the sidewalk and children have no bedtimes
in summer. Take him to your favorite auntie's
house. Let him get a tongue lashing from your
Hotep cousin while you "help" in the kitchen
by taste-testing quinoa salad/arroz con pollo/
collard greens.

5.
So, your white boy has fallen in love with you.
He has told off Johnnie Come Woke-ly friends,
but he is asking whether it might be easier with
someone browner than him, whether your parents,
your best friend, your abuelita would be happier.
Hold his hands in yours. Notice his red face, tear-
filled eyes. Tell him the truth.

I Could Almost Mistake
This Gold Peninsula for Gospel

As morning's first fishermen nestle
poles in sand, searching for hungry

mouths, pelicans fly single file, wingtips
stirring surf. Black-headed gulls

are more polite than their northern
cousins—only speaking when spoken

to. Clouds tower against dawn's pink
innards. The white family with white

dogs ambles down shore. The mother
smiles hard and wide for the black

girlfriend her son has brought on family
vacation. Right now, I would rather write

pelicans than people. This among my many
sins: an inability to look at the thing itself,

refusing surprise. But I cannot ignore this
fellow bespectacled brown girl, resplendent

in box braids, how she holds her boyfriend's
hand, sliding her fingers between his over and
over; one hand jetty, the other, water.

Oyá Fucks Cúchulainn

Of course, the gods use Tinder. We swipe in all four
cardinal directions—heavens, underworld, right, left.

I only wanted to make Changó cringe, to make him
want our thunder again. I thought this white boy
would make him rage for my wind, whip, and holler
instead of Ochun's smooth hips. I set my GPS for Ulster.

I liked this one's voice—the way his sentences rolled
across green hills. I didn't expect him to have such
soft hands. But want is impractical.

He called me princess the whole night. I tried to leave
under the cover of darkness, but he pouted, told me
he wanted to show me a new world, how I would be
worshiped across the sea at sunrise.

He had already gathered fresh honey for breakfast.
I thought of Changó's power—his laughter, the sheen
of his skin, his dance that makes even the earth shudder
with pleasure. But he ain't made breakfast in years.
I watched the sunrise and headed home, speeding
back across the Atlantic.

I know Emer might be pissed, but this wasn't about love,
girl. Just need. That deep desire to know you can still get
it if you want.

After the Argument

I go for a midnight walk.
Christmas lights fumble
into Valentine decor.
Children are still whining
behind lit windows.

Being a woman walking
at midnight, I try to appear
ruggedly male in knit cap,
puffer coat. Being black walking
at midnight, I try not to look
too threatening, whistle some
Beethoven or Fleetwood Mac.

I walk anger and sorrow. I walk
wasted years and good times. I
walk the times I said yes and meant
no. I want to make *no* a mantra.
I want to only say yes to myself
for a little while.

I circle the block, ignore his texts
under a waxing moon. I have left
the porch light on for myself. I
write rage on my phone. *No replacements*

found appears when I misspell words
in fury. So I let autofill take over:
i'll be there in the morning.

i'll be there in the morning.

The Black Duchess

Said that she uses Dr. Bronner's soap
and has tea tree oil in her bag, black
hippie swag. She has a bad relationship
with her dad. "I should be the one walking
you down the aisle," said her mama, just as
my mama did. The black duchess is just like
us: indeterminately black girls who have been
asked "where are you from?" knowing the answer
sought wasn't *Texas* or *Queens, New Jersey* or the *South Side.*

Men around us say, *who cares about a wedding, about monarchy,*
about this pasty-ass family adding a member whose ancestors
they oppressed? This is some neocolonial bullshit.
They cross their arms and huff as we wake early
to watch the car pull up with the black bride,
to see her mother's locs tucked under a tear-
shaped mint green fascinator, to see her mother's
nose ring gleam. We watch the black bishop,
the black choir.

We watch for our ancestors who were mistresses
to white men, those who hid their black mothers
so they could enter the chapel, so they could live
their dim and hollow fairytale. We watch because
until 1967 this was illegal in the princess's home state,
because of boyfriends who said, *I love you, but I have*

to marry a white girl or my grandparents will cut me off, but
you understand, don't you? because a single black mother
was wearing green and so was the queen, because we
wish she wouldn't straighten her hair, because we wish
we could get a blowout like that, because the first
interracial kiss on tv was only because aliens made Uhura
and Kirk do it, because we've always had a soft spot
for gingers, because she doesn't cover her freckles
with makeup, because she is divorced, because she,
too, tiptoes toward forty, because the duchess gave her
own damn self away.

Consistency

When the ponytailed girl behind the counter
at the coffee shop says, *I want to have somebody
next to me in bed and just read every night—then
I'll know I've made it,* we share a glance. *I guess
we made it,* I say and we laugh, you, me, and
the ponytail.

How easy it is to lose sight of what I, what
we have. When we reach for our books or
devices instead of each other, thumbing
through pages—never glancing at each
other at the same time—you laughing
at a tweet, email, or whatever until
I have to ask you: *what? What?*

Sometimes

My mother is divorcing ~~my stepfather~~ her husband. It's been
thirty-six years since she divorced ~~her first husband~~ my father. I am
the only child to emerge from my mother and father's relationship.
My ~~mother's two other children my half~~ siblings will have each other
to process this experience with their father. In college I used to tell
myself that home was wherever ~~my bed sheets and suitcase lay~~. Now
I tell myself that home is where my husband ~~and cats are~~ is. We have
been married a dozen years. Sometimes I am tremendously happy
in my marriage. Sometimes I am unhappy. Sometimes I threaten
divorce in my unhappiness. Whenever I make these threats, ~~I feel
regret~~. I know how manipulative it is to threaten. I have a house and
am married to a person I love, ~~but I still strain for an unreachable
idea of home~~. My very cells ~~are afraid of what happens when I~~ cling
to what seems like a sure thing for too long.

wanderer lay your
head on pine needle pillows
make the stars your roof

Carolina Beach

On the pier, under a waltz of light, couples shuffle
toward the pink neon bar sign advertising half-off
pitchers and Sunday morning services.

Tonight, the moon is a cross section of elephant tusk
lighting a silver path from horizon to shore—
push/pull satellite in full effect.

You dump boiled crabs on the newspapered
table. We crack carapace. We suck sweetness
from knuckle and claw.

V

Date of Last Period

The first time I had my period, we had burnt
beef patties and broccoli for dinner. Blood
came as a surprise—and not. All the other
girls in my grade had already bled. The cheery
red on my white cotton underwear readmitted
me to their ranks.

Over dinner, my mom explained pregnancy:
endgame of this bleeding between my legs.
Terrified of tearing as she'd described, I kept
my legs closed for the next seven years—no
glimpses, not a finger. Even tampons threatened
the flower. It took a team of three girls outside
a stall door barking instructions—*tilt back, put
one foot on the edge of the seat*—before
anything could enter.

The first night I didn't get my period, I don't
remember what I ate. He and I talked about
whether this was what we wanted under a dim
pendant lamp over the kitchen table. I decided
on pills. I remember feeling my body readjust—
that swaying at boat's bottom, that gentle watery
nausea. I remember mucus and, finally, the joy
blood brought: bright red with clots the color
of crushed violets.

Mary's Song

Praise the doctor's hands,
anesthesia, suction,
the body's subtle amnesia.

I will shed a few
and fit into that blue
prom dress, that black
racer-back swim-team Speedo.

I will cut through
the water,
and no one
will ever know.

When You Ask Why
My Arms Are Empty

Why, on this march toward forty, my man
and I live in a house with more bedrooms
than bodies, I say I'm not ready, I say art
is reproduction, that I teach—so don't I
already have so many children to love?

What I cannot say: I was twelve, the only
one home. My mother wept on the throne.
I begged her to let me call for an ambulance,
but she shook her head between sobs, held
my hand as our bathroom filled with blood's
copper scent. She held out a tissue to me with
something pink, only little larger than my thumb:
This was your brother. Oh god oh god oh—

Puerto Vallarta

It is dark. The ocean swells and crashes. A half-dozen sister sea
turtles pull themselves onto the shore. Their approach is a slow
flippered shuffle. Each finds a place to dig a cavity in the dry sand,
sending up plumes of sediment. This one seems to cry as she
releases her eggs. She shovels and beats the sand back into place.
The beach vibrates with her flippers' thwack.

> Moonless summer night
> one hundred moons buried
> deep in earth's womb

Thirteen Ways of
Looking at a Bathroom

i.
The full moon is rising.
The bathroom is occupied.

ii.
When you're asked what you're doing
in the bathroom, the right answer
is *nothing, be right out.*

iii.
Three yellow butterfly decals
on the bathroom mirror hold
the triangle of broken glass in place.

iv.
A mosquito attempts to enter the pink
bathroom through the window's mesh
screen. On the windowsill lies a dead beetle
with orange wings.

v.
Pimples I pop in the bathroom mirror aren't
as bad as the dark scars they leave behind.

vi.
I sift through my mother's abandoned
hair products in the bathroom: pump
out a puff of orange-scented mousse,
blow it into the sink.

vii.
*Why would you want to relax that wonderful
hair?* My hair spirals from my scalp, rising
into humidity. In the bathroom mirror, I
brush it back.

viii.
In the bathroom, like the kitchen, there
is olive oil—a bottle for pots,
a bottle for my hair.

ix.
In the bathroom, I discover my vulva,
layered brown and pink, a new country
in the aqua hand mirror.

x.
Through the bathroom's sheer curtains,
a view of the yard of our rented house
and an obese cat stretched out in the sun.

xi.
Here in the bathroom, elbows find
Vaseline and cocoa butter to soothe
ashy skin back to brown.

xii.
I dream of a viper ready to strike.
He dances on the toilet seat while
I back out of the bathroom.

xiii.
She leaves the bathroom;
the vapor leaves with her.

This is my body—

naked arms   sagging jowl
    knuckle pop
cystic breast   tilted uterus

when I have stood naked before mirrors
                  when I have twisted before mirrors
both pleased and mortified by my abominable
body   firmness giving way to wrinkles   pimples
                to chin hair   dust to dust

I've wished my body invisible   as if
this were possible for a woman with my face
in this country

when I wish I had not said what I've said
(which is most of the time when I say)

I wish for my body to fold in on itself
my bones rice paper
until I am small enough to slide
into pocket until I am small enough
to disappear into the eververnal continuum
luminous
                broken for you

Hadeology

Gravity is the weakest force,
but it can bring a body down.

An adjunct professor on concrete outside of a church
A hood entrepreneur on concrete outside a three-story walkup
A schizophrenic son on concrete outside of his mother's apartment
A recent high school grad on a bathroom floor
A biking single mother and an eighteen-wheeler
A college student and his father's gun

Trillium
Cornflower
Aster
Honeysuckle
Poinsettia
Wild cane

We are electrons bound by nuclear pull,
magnetism. We spin out of orbit
and are pulled back a thousand times a day.

I only learned today what makes a glass
of water grow stale overnight. The obvious:
dissolved gasses. The strange:
the presence of geosmin—
molecule that scents earth after rain.

As the former outermost planet,
Pluto once had my complete affection,
but things change. Casey Goodson Jr.
did not get to inspect his newly cleansed
smile upon returning home. A good son,
he carried a bag of sandwiches home.

Last year, a woman I know taught
me a Turkish recipe for the purslane
growing wild in my front yard. This
year, the purslane did not return.
Instead, another woman friend told
me to make tea from the rosemary
growing rampant. Something always
springs back. Gravity is fickle, after all.

Gathering Ingredients for Sancocho
in Appalachia during the Pandemic

I find plátanos easily enough.
I can do without cassava, but no one
here has heard of chayote, even after
I learn the ugly English word for it.

It's not that I like the bland vegetable
pear, but it is vital in its greenness,
its refusal to soften and melt away
into the stew, how it stands up to sofrito.

My mother's sancocho has chunks of chayote
so big, I cut them with my spoon just to fit
them into my mouth.

I have not felt my mother's hands
for fifteen months. I could not go home
when my stepfather was gasping.

I get my first vaccine. I make my sancocho
with zucchini and butternut squash.
It tastes almost the way I remember.

Street Corner Market, Philadelphia

I spot the gold fruit piled high in green paper baskets,
can't help the *oooo* that spills as I reach toward them.
The mumu-ed woman standing in front of me turns,

saying, *The smell brings me back to Virginia.* High yellow,
plum-round, she tells me fields her granddaddy owned,
sold, meadows she girled through. We talk counties—

Carolina, Henrico—we talk tobacco, sunflower seed; we
speak of what hung in those orchards. Though I've only
known that land through car windows on visits to kin,

and my orchards were city parks, mulberries fermenting
on concrete, something in me understands the honey of child
in field. She says, *I was home today, watching TV and craving some*

sweet, some fresh, you know? We dare one another to bite into
our bounty before parting. Our teeth score skin, juice racing
rivulets toward elbows. We give ourselves over to sweet.

Acknowledgments

With appreciation to Annie Finch, who included a version of "Date of Last Period" in the anthology *Choice Words: Writers on Abortion* and with gratitude to the editors of the following journals who first published earlier versions of the following poems:

The Acentos Review
"Eight Minutes, Forty-Six Seconds"
"lighting candles on my stoop/watching the wind snuff them out,"

Alaska Quarterly Review
"Street Corner Market, Philadelphia"

Anomaly
"Boondocks:"

Black Renaissance Noire
"Little Church"
"Fly"

Cincinnati Review
"Spring Semester"

Cherry Tree
"Aerodynamics"

Cortland Review
"Carolina Beach"

Crazyhorse
"Appalachia → LGA"
"Monongahela Means Falling"

Diode Poetry Journal
"Skin"
"Inheritance"

Huizache
"On Flying Over the Border Wall"
"An Old White Woman Touched My Hair at Rising Creek Bakery"

Lily Poetry Review
"Cebu City"

Mass Poetry
"Gathering Ingredients for Sancocho in Appalachia the Pandemic"

Missouri Review
"149th Street"

New Guard Review
"Hood Aesthetic"
"Easter 1986"

New Ohio Review
"Chiba"

Obsidian
"Queensborough"

Ploughshares
"Hadeology"

PRISM international
"I Could Almost Mistake This Gold Peninsula for Gospel"

Rattle
"How to Date a White Boy"
"When You Ask Why My Arms are Empty"

River Styx
"Jíbara Negra"

Salamander
"Gloria, In Excelsis"

Sou'wester
"In Virginia,"
"CPR"

Storm Cellar
"Sometimes"

Sugar House Review
"Polaris"

TIMBER
"Shaped into a Kind of Life"
"This is my body—"

The Wide Shore: A Journal of Global Women's Poetry
"Dominant/recessive"
"Eleggua"

Notes

"Appalachia→ LGA": This poem is in conversation with Tiana Clark's "BNA→ LAX." The Redbird trains referenced here ran from Queens to Manhattan and back for all my young life. The last Redbird ran the line in 2003. In the same year, these train cars were sunk off the East Coast of the United States, creating an artificial reef.

"Dominant/recessive": The quotation in the third stanza comes directly from the diary of Christopher Columbus/Cristóbal Colón, regarding his impressions of the Taino.

"Monongahela Means Falling": Arthur Bagenda was a Ugandan American university student. He was two months away from twenty when his body was found near the Walnut Steet Bridge in Morgan-town, West Virginia. His death remains unsolved. His life mattered.

"In Virginia,": On my first visit to Virginia, it was autumn, there was mist, and I felt the presence of Black women attempting to escape toward freedom at the edges of the fields. I don't believe in ghosts, but there are ghosts in the Piedmont.

"On the Futility of Pouring Water on a Dying Dolphin": This poem was written on July 10, 2015, in North Carolina. On this day, three hours away, the confederate flag was officially removed from the South Carolina state house, less than two weeks after activist Bree Newsome scaled the flagpole to take it down.

About the Author

Amy M. Alvarez's work has appeared in *Ploughshares*, the *Missouri Review*, *Cincinnati Review*, and elsewhere. She is also the coeditor of *Essential Voices: A COVID-19 Anthology* (2023). Amy has been awarded fellowships from CantoMundo, VONA, Macondo, Virginia Center for the Creative Arts, and the Furious Flower Poetry Center. Amy was born in New York City to Jamaican and Puerto Rican parents. She taught English, history, and humanities courses at public high schools in the Bronx, New York, and Roxbury, Massachusetts. She has taught writing at various institutions, most recently West Virginia University. In 2022, she was inducted as an Affrilachian Poet.